SCHIRMER'S LIBRARY
OF MUSICAL CLASSICS

JOHANN SEBASTIAN BACH

English Suites

For the Piano

After the edition of

KARL CZERNY

Book I — Library Vol. 17

→ Book II — Library Vol. 18

G. SCHIRMER, Inc.

DISTRIBUTED BY

HAL•LEONARD®
CORPORATION

7777 W. BLUEMOUND RD. P.O. BOX 13819 MILWAUKEE, WI 53213

Contents.

————————•◦•◦•◦————————

Embellishments.
(les Agréments.)

| Inverted Mordent. | Mordent. | Trill without after-beat. | Trill with after-beat. |

Thematic Index

Suite IV.

Prelude.

Allegro moderato.($\quad$=100)

Piano.

Allemande.

Allegro moderato. ($\bullet$ = 88)

Courante.

Molto Allegro. (♩ = 96)

Sarabande.

Andante sostenuto. ($\quad$ = 60)

Menuet I.

Andante con moto. ($\sf{\downarrow}$ = 116)

Menuet II.

Menuet I D.C.

Gigue.

Presto. (♩. = 144)

Suite V.

Prelude.

Allegro.(♪.= 72)

Allemande.

Allegro moderato. (♩ = 84)

Courante.

Allegro vivace.($\downarrow$ = 88)

Sarabande.
Andante. ($\quad$ = 63)

Passepied I.
(in Rondo-form.)
Allegretto vivace. (♩.= 66)

Passepied II.

Passepied I D.C.

Gigue.

Allegro. (♩.=80)

Suite VI.

Prelude.
Lento. (♩. = 66)

Allemande.

Lento moderato. ($\bullet$ = 76)

Courante.

Allegro vivace. ($\mathbf{d}$ = 92)

Sarabande.

Andante con moto. ($\mathtt{d}$ = 60)

Double.

Gavotte I.

Allegro vivace. (♩ = 80)

il basso sempre legato.

Gavotte II.
(or the Musette.)

Gavotte I da capo.

Gigue.

Allegro. (♪ = 132)